SCIENCE FACTORY

UNITS &
MEASUREMENTS

JON RICHARDS

COPPER BEECH BOOKS
BROOKFIELD, CONNECTICUT

© Aladdin Books Ltd 2000

Designed and produced by
Aladdin Books Ltd
28 Percy Street
London W1P 0LD

First published in the United States
in 2000 by
Copper Beech Books, an imprint of
The Millbrook Press
2 Old New Milford Road
Brookfield, Connecticut 06804

Editor
Kathy Gemmell

Design
David West
Children's Book Design

Designer
Jennifer Skelly

Illustrator
Ian Moores

Printed in Belgium

ISBN 0-7613-1158-0

Cataloging-in-Publication Data is on
file at the Library of Congress.

The author, Jon Richards, has written
a number of science and technology
books for children.

The consultant, Steve Parker, has
worked on over 150 books for
children, mainly on a science theme.

All the photos in this book were
taken by Roger Vlitos.

INTRODUCTION

Everything we do, everything we see, and everywhere we go can be measured in one kind of unit or another. Measuring in units lets you compare one distance with another, and helps you figure out how far away, or how heavy, an object is. It also tells you how long it takes you to do something. You can even measure the wind! Read on and discover a host of projects to teach you more about measuring.

CONTENTS

YOUR FACTORY
Hints and tips
on how to prepare for your projects.
pages 4-5

HOW FAR?
Make a measuring
wheel to see how far
apart objects are.
pages 6-7

FINDING THE ANGLE
Make a theodolite to
measure the angles of slopes.
pages 8-9

GRID LOCK
Find the area of shapes using a grid.
pages 10-11

SPILLING OVER
Use water to find out the volume
of different objects.
pages 12-13

FLOATING AND SINKING
Measure the density of different liquids.
pages 14-15

LIGHT AND HEAVY
Build a weighing machine.
pages 16-17

IN THE BALANCE
Make a set of scales from
a coat hanger.
pages 18-19

FINDING THE MIDDLE
Find the center of gravity
of a shape using
a plumb line.
pages 20-21

THE SANDS OF TIME
Make an hourglass.
pages 22-23

SWING TIME
Learn to measure time
more accurately with a
pendulum clock.
pages 24-25

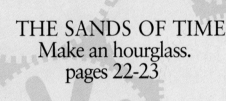

MEASURING SPEED
Make a wind-speed reader
to measure the wind.
pages 26-27

GETTING FASTER
Measure how a car rolls faster
on a steeper slope.
pages 28-29

FINDING OUT MORE
Interesting phrases and mind-blowing
facts about measuring.
pages 30-31

INDEX
page 32

YOUR FACTORY

BEFORE YOU START any of the projects, it is important that you learn a few simple rules about the care of your science factory.

● Always keep your hands and the work surfaces clean. Dirt can damage results and ruin a project.

● Read the instructions very carefully before you start each project.

● Make sure you have all the equipment you need for the project (see checklist opposite).

● If you haven't got the right piece of equipment, then improvise. For example, a liquid detergent bottle will do just as well as a plastic drink bottle.

● Don't be afraid to make mistakes. Just start again – patience is very important!

Equipment checklist:
- Toothpicks and wooden sticks
- Cardboard box and shoe box
- Drinking straws
- Plastic drink bottles and transparent beakers
- Water, salt, oil, and vinegar
- Scissors, tape, and glue
- Ruler, protractor, and compass
- Small container and large bowl
- Measuring jug and food coloring
- Felt-tip markers, pencil, and paints
- Thumbtacks, nails, and paper fasteners
- Toy car, battery, and other small objects
- Paper, stiff cardboard, colored cardboard, and plastic film
- Cork, corkboard, and piece of wood
- Cotton thread, elastic band, and string
- Table-tennis ball
- Modeling clay
- Watch or clock
- Coat hanger

WARNING:
Some of the projects in this book need the help of an adult. Always ask a grown-up to give you a hand when you are using scissors or sharp objects such as nails.

HOW FAR?

HOW FAR DO YOU HAVE TO TRAVEL to school each day? How long is your bedroom? How far away is your favorite store? All of these questions are about distance. To measure distance, we use units such as inches, feet, and even miles. Build a measuring wheel in this project and see how you can measure the distance between objects.

WHAT YOU NEED
Ruler
String
Thumbtack
Pencil
Colored cardboard
Nail
Wooden stick
Cork, Tape
Glue

SMALLER WHEEL

Use string just under 3 inches long to make another circle 18 inches around its edge. This gives a more exact reading than your first wheel, because smaller units are more accurate.

5 *To measure the distance between two objects, start with your wheel next to the first object, with the arrow pointing to the ground. Roll it to the second object in a straight line. Count how many times the arrow touches the ground before you reach the second object – this will give you the distance between the objects in yards.*

MEASURING WHEEL

1 Cut a piece of string just under 6 inches long. Tie the pencil to one end and pin the other end onto the middle of the piece of cardboard. Then draw a circle using the pencil. Ask an adult to cut the circle out.

2 Cut out an arrow shape and glue it to your circle. Point the tip of the arrow toward the edge of the circle, and the base toward the center of the circle (where the thumbtack was).

3 Tape the nail across one end of the stick, as shown. Wrap more tape around the stick to hold the first piece of tape in place.

WHY IT WORKS

Making the radius of the circle (the distance from the center to the edge) just under 6 inches makes the distance around the edge about 1 yard. The wheel goes around once for every yard covered. So the number of times it goes around equals the number of yards between the objects.

1 YARD

4 Push the nail through the center of the circle. Push the cork onto the nail. Make sure the wheel can still turn.

FINDING THE ANGLE

When mapping out a piece of land, surveyors not only need to find out the distance between points, but also the steepness of any slope, called the gradient. You may have seen surveyors at work using an instrument on a tripod called a theodolite. This tells them the angle, up or down, from where they are standing to another piece of ground. Make a simple theodolite in this project.

WHAT YOU NEED
Colored cardboard
Glue, Scissors
Ruler
Protractor
Battery
String
Tape

MEASURING HEIGHT

Surveyors also use theodolites to calculate the height of objects. By finding out the angle to the top of an object and the distance to the object from where they are standing, surveyors use simple mathematics to find out the object's height.

4 *To measure the angle between where you are and another object, simply look at the object through the two viewers. Ask somebody to read off the angle between the string and the center 0° line of the theodolite. This is the angle between you and the object.*

THEODOLITE

1 Using the method shown on page 7, draw and cut out a circle of cardboard. Cut it in half. Using the protractor and ruler, mark lines at 10° intervals. Number the lines, from 0° in the middle to 90° at either end of the flat edge.

90°

— 90°

2 Make two viewers by rolling two narrow strips of cardboard into loops. Sandwich these loops between the two semicircles of cardboard and glue them all together.

3 Ask an adult to help you cover the battery with cardboard, as shown. Tape the battery to a piece of string 24 inches long to make a plumb line. Tape the other end of the string to the center of the flat edge of the semicircle. You have now made a theodolite.

0°

WHY IT WORKS

As you raise or lower the flat edge to line it up with an object, the plumb line swings to an angle away from the 0° line. This angle is the same as the angle between yourself and the object.

0°

25°

GRID LOCK

ANOTHER MEASUREMENT surveyors often need is the amount of land something covers. This is called the area of an object. Area can be measured in a wide range of units, including acres, square inches, square feet, square yards, and square miles. Some areas are easy to find. For a square, you simply multiply the length of one side by itself. This project shows you how to find the area of simple and complicated shapes.

WHAT YOU NEED
*Sheet of plastic film, Ruler
Felt-tip marker
Colored cardboard
Scissors*

SMALLER GRID

Make a grid with squares that are only 0.5 in. across and use it to measure the area of shapes. You will find that you can measure the areas more exactly than with the larger-sized grid.

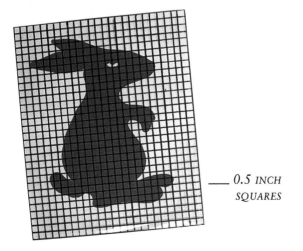

— *0.5 INCH SQUARES*

FINDING THE AREA

1 *Ask an adult to cut out different shapes from colored cardboard. Cut out simple shapes such as squares and rectangles, and more complex ones such as circles or animal shapes.*

2 *Using the ruler and the felt-tip marker, measure half-inch intervals along the edges of the plastic film. Join opposite points on the edges to form a grid of squares, each ½ inch by ½ inch.*

WHY IT WORKS

By breaking a shape up into squares, you can see the area it covers. If you ignore the less-than-half-covered squares, you can count each more-than-half-covered square as one full square. Test this by drawing a rectangle and placing the grid over it. Count the squares, then move the grid slightly. Count again, using the rule for partially covered squares. You will get the same result both times.

3 Put the grid over a shape and count the number of whole grid squares that cover the shape.

4 Now count the squares that are more than half covered, and add that to the whole squares. This gives you the area of your shape in square inches.

11

SPILLING OVER

WITH DISTANCE AND AREA, you have measured units in one and two dimensions. The amount of space an object takes up in three dimensions is called its volume. As with area, you can use simple math formulae to work out the volume of some objects – the volume of a box can be found by multiplying its base by its height by its depth. This project shows how to find the volume of any object.

WHAT YOU NEED
Cardboard box
Scissors, Glue
Colored cardboard
Two wooden sticks
Small container
Large bowl
Water
Measuring jug
Small objects

FINDING THE VOLUME

1 To make a stand, ask an adult to cut out the sides of a cardboard box. The box must be wide enough to slide the large bowl in and out.

2 To decorate the stand, cut out strips of colored cardboard. Glue the strips to the sides and top of the stand.

3 Place the sticks over your stand and balance the small container on them. Place the large bowl underneath. Fill the small container to the brim with water. Be careful not to spill water into the large bowl.

IN THE BATH

With a water-based marker, mark the level of a bath before you get in. As you get in, the level rises. Like the object in the container, your body displaces an amount of water equal to its volume.

4 Gently place an object into the small container.

5 Watch as the water spills over into the large bowl.

6 Pour the water in the large bowl into a measuring jug.

7 Put the jug on a flat surface and read off how much water is in it. This is the volume of the object you put in the container.

WHY IT WORKS

When you place the object into the small container of water, it pushes out, or displaces, a volume of water that equals its own volume. You can then measure this volume of water by pouring it into a measuring jug.

OBJECT

WATER DISPLACED BY OBJECT

FLOATING AND SINKING

WHEN A TRAIN IS FULL OF PASSENGERS, we say that the people are closely, or densely, packed inside. In the same way, the tiny molecules that make up substances can be more densely packed in some objects than in others. This project shows you how to make a hydrometer that allows you to test and compare the densities of different liquids.

HYDROMETER

1 *Ask an adult to cut a length of straw. Put a ball of clay on one end to make a hydrometer.*

2 *Fill a beaker with a certain amount of water. Using the felt-tip marker, mark on the straw the water level at which the straw floats.*

3 *Pour out the same amounts of vinegar, oil, and salt water as the original water. Put in the hydrometer and see at what level it floats.*

WHY IT WORKS

The density of a liquid depends upon the size of the molecules that make it up, as well as how tightly packed they are. Oil has very big molecules compared to water, but these oil molecules are not as tightly packed together. In fact, they are quite spread out. So water, with its more closely packed molecules, is more dense than oil. The straw will therefore sink farther in oil than in water.

WATER MOLECULES

OIL MOLECULES

4 Look at how the hydrometer floats higher in denser liquids, such as salt water, but lower in less dense liquids, such as oil.

SETTLING IN LAYERS

Carefully pour liquids of different densities into the same transparent beaker. They will settle into different bands, with the most dense liquid sitting on the bottom of the beaker and the least dense liquid floating on the top.

LIGHT AND HEAVY

YOU MAY HAVE SEEN HOW ASTRONAUTS in space float around their spacecraft. They have no weight because they are so far from the Earth, and moving so fast, that they are not affected by its gravity. On the Earth's surface, we feel weight because weight is the combination of an object's density and the effect of the Earth's gravity. This project shows you how to compare the weight of different objects.

WHAT YOU NEED
Ruler
Felt-tip marker
Stiff cardboard
Plastic bottle
Paints
Scissors
Cotton thread
Piece of wood
Elastic band
Toothpick
Two nails

WEIGHING IT UP

1 *Use the ruler and felt-tip marker to mark out a scale along one edge of a strip of cardboard.*

2 *Ask an adult to cut the bottom off the plastic bottle to make a basket. Paint the basket. Ask an adult to pierce two holes near the top of the basket. Tie the thread through these holes.*

3 *Decorate the top of the plastic bottle using the paint. Ask an adult to cut a small flap into its base. This flap will hold the top of the bottle in place against the piece of wood.*

4 *Tie the elastic band to the thread on the basket. Loop the other end of the elastic band over the neck of the bottle. Attach the toothpick to the base of the basket to act as a pointer.*

5 Put the piece of wood in an upright position and place the strip of cardboard against it. Ask an adult to secure the top of the bottle to the top of the piece of wood by knocking the two nails through the flap. Mark on the scale where the toothpick rests when the basket is empty.

WHY IT WORKS

The Earth's gravity attracts objects downward. The heavier any object placed in the basket is, the more it weighs and the more it stretches the elastic band.

HEAVY OBJECT

LIGHT OBJECT

6 Test the weight of different objects by placing them in the basket. Heavy objects will cause the elastic band to stretch a lot and the basket to hang low down on the scale. Lighter weights will rest higher on the scale.

WEIGHING IN WATER

Take the elastic band and basket off the bottle top. Put an object in the basket and see how far it stretches the elastic band. Now lower the basket into a bucket of water. What happens to the basket and the elastic band? Is the elastic band still stretched by the same amount?

IN THE BALANCE

THE PREVIOUS PROJECT SHOWED you how to compare the weights of different objects one after the other. But the weight of an object can have another purpose. If you have an object that you know the weight of, you can use it to find the weight of other objects using an instrument called a balance. This project shows you how to make a simple balance.

BALANCING ACT

1 Ask an adult to pierce two holes in each beaker, one on either side near the top. Tie string to these holes to form long hoops.

2 Draw a scale on the cardboard using the marker and ruler. Make the central line longer so it stands out.

3 Tape the drinking straw to the underside of the coat hanger so that it points down.

4 Hang one beaker on each arm of the hanger and check that they are level when the hanger is hung up by its hook. Place the scale behind the hanger so the middle line sits behind the straw when the beakers are empty.

WHY IT WORKS

The hanger is a pivot around which the weights of the objects act. If the objects in the right-hand beaker weigh more, they exert more force on the coat hanger, causing the right side to hang lower.

RIGHT-HAND BEAKER WEIGHS MORE

5 Compare the weights of different objects by placing them in each basket. See how much you need of different substances, such as water and sugar, before they balance.

COMPARING WEIGHTS

Get two objects which are the same size, but weigh different amounts, such as a tennis ball and a baseball. Place them in the beakers. The baseball will tip the balance because it is more dense.

FINDING THE MIDDLE

EVERY OBJECT HAS A CENTER OF GRAVITY. This is an imaginary point through which the weight of the object acts. In the last project, you saw how, by pivoting the coat hanger around its center of gravity, you were able to make it balance. At any other place, the pivot would not have been in line with the coat hanger's center of gravity, and would not have balanced. This project will show you how to find the center of gravity for any flat shape.

WHAT YOU NEED
Corkboard
Stiff cardboard
Scissors
Thumbtack
String
Modeling clay
Ruler
Pencil

CENTER OF GRAVITY

1 *Ask an adult to cut out a random shape from the piece of cardboard.*

2 *Push one end of a length of string into a lump of modeling clay. Stick the thumbtack through the other end and push it through the cardboard shape. Pin the shape to the corkboard, making sure it can swing freely.*

5 *Test your shape's center of gravity by balancing a sharp pencil upright, using modeling clay. Carefully place the shape on the pencil point where the lines cross. The shape will balance.*

When the string hangs from the same point as the cardboard, it passes through the cardboard's center of gravity. This is because weight always acts vertically down toward the center of the Earth.

CENTER OF GRAVITY

3 Using the ruler, draw along the line made by the string as it hangs. Repeat a few times, pinning the shape in a different place each time.

4 You will notice that the lines cross in one spot. This spot is the shape's center of gravity.

FANCY SHAPES

Cut out complex shapes from cardboard. Use the same method to find their center of gravity. Each time you pin the shapes, pin them as close to the edges as you can.

THE SANDS OF TIME

THERE IS ONE UNIT that is being used continuously and requires measuring all the time – and that's time! For thousands of years, people have measured the passing of time, using more and more complex methods to get more and more accurate readings. One of the earliest forms of time measurer, or clock, was the hourglass. This project shows you how to make your own simple hourglass.

WHAT YOU NEED
Two small bottles
Cardboard
Sharp pencil
Table salt
Watch or clock

HOURGLASS

2 *Pour some salt into the other bottle.*

1 *Make a tube from a strip of cardboard that will fit snugly over the necks of the bottles. Slide it over the top of one bottle. Ask an adult to cut out a small circle of cardboard to cover the mouth of the bottle and to make a small hole in the middle with a sharp pencil. Put the circle inside the tube so it covers the mouth of the bottle.*

3 *Turn the bottle with the tube upside-down and slide it over the mouth of the bottle containing the salt. Check the cardboard tube fits snugly.*

4 *Turn the bottles over, so the bottle with the salt is on top. The salt will start pouring into the bottom bottle.*

5 Using a watch or clock, time how long it takes for all the salt to flow from one bottle to the next. When this has happened, turn the bottles over and repeat. You will find that the time is exactly the same.

WHY IT WORKS

Gravity makes the salt fall into the bottom bottle. The flow of salt is slowed by the small hole which the salt has to pass through. As the amount of salt and the size of the hole remain the same, the time it takes the salt to flow from one bottle to the next will stay the same, however many times you repeat the project.

TIME RUNNING OUT

Make another form of timekeeper using a cardboard funnel, shown here. This time, mark lines on the side of the bottle. Read off where the top of the pile of salt is after each minute.

SWING TIME

TIME IS MEASURED BY SMALLER and smaller units, from years to months, to days, to hours, to seconds, and even to millionths of a second. The hourglass you made on pages 22-23 can be useful for measuring periods of time of about a minute, but it doesn't work for very small periods of time. One solution is to use a pendulum clock. This relies on the regular swing of a weight on the end of a length of string or wire, called a pendulum.

WHAT YOU NEED
Cardboard box
Wooden sticks
Cardboard
Modeling clay
Tape
Small tack
Drinking straw
Paints

TICK TOCK

1 *Ask an adult to make a hole in the middle of one side of the cardboard box, as shown. Draw and then cut out a clock face the same width as the box.*

2 *Tape the face to the side of the box. Ask an adult to push a small stick through the base of the face. Tape the rest of the stick to the box.*

3 *Decorate your clock. Mark a scale on the clock face so you can check the pendulum's swing.*

4 *For the pendulum, attach a circle of cardboard and a lump of modeling clay to one end of a long stick.*

5 *On the other end, attach a short length of stick with a circle of cardboard stuck to each end.*

6 *Make a pointer from the straw and a triang of cardboard. Ask an adu to attach the pointer to the top of the pendulum*

7 Ask an adult to tack the pendulum to the piece of wood sticking out from the clock face. Put the clock on the edge of a table, so the pendulum swings freely.

WHY IT WORKS

The length of time a pendulum takes to swing is determined by the length of the string, or, in this case, the stick. As the pendulum swings, friction from the air and friction on the pivot tack slow its movement and also lessen the distance of each swing. As a result, each swing takes the same amount of time, no matter what distance the pendulum swings.

8 Swing the pendulum. Each swing takes the same time, no matter how far the pendulum moves.

TIME YOUR SWING

The swing time of your pendulum is governed by the length of the wooden stick. If the stick is shorter, it will swing faster, and if it is longer, it will swing slower. Alter the length of the stick so that each swing takes one second. Check with a watch.

MEASURING SPEED

WHAT YOU NEED
Compass
Felt-tip marker
Scissors
Stiff cardboard
*Table-tennis
ball*
Thumbtack
Tape

THE SPEED OF THINGS is referred to in several places in this book. In the previous project, the speed of the pendulum as it swings is an important factor in determining how long each swing takes. Speed is the rate at which a distance is covered. This project shows how you can compare the different speeds of the air as it moves around you – what we call wind.

WIND SPEED

1 *Draw a curved scale onto cardboard using the compass and the felt-tip marker. Mark equal points on the scale so you can compare wind speeds.*

2 *Ask an adult to cut out a strip of cardboard with a small window in it so you can see the scale.*

WATCH THE WINDOW

Make another wind-speed measurer by tying strips of thick cardboard, thin cardboard, tin foil, paper, and tissue paper to a stick, in that order. Start with the thick cardboard at the bottom. A weak wind will only move the tissue paper, but it will take a strong wind to move all the strips including the thick one.

3 *Tape the table-tennis ball to one end of the cardboard strip. Pin the other end of the strip onto the sheet of cardboard on the spot where the point of the compass made a small hole. Make sure the strip can swing freely.*

4 Hold your wind-speed reader in a windy spot and see how far the cardboard strip is pushed when the wind blows.

WHY IT WORKS

When the wind blows on the table-tennis ball, the moving air pushes the ball. The faster the wind blows, the more the table-tennis ball is pushed, and the farther up the scale the cardboard arm moves.

WIND

GETTING FASTER

WHAT YOU NEED
Toy car
Shoe box
Stiff cardboard
Scissors
Plastic bottle
Paper fastener
Paper, Tape
Protractor
Ruler
Water
Felt-tip marker
Food coloring

FROM THE PREVIOUS PROJECT you will have seen that the wind can blow at different speeds. This change of speed is called acceleration if it is getting faster, and deceleration if it is getting slower. This project shows you how different rates of acceleration can be caused by changes in the angle of a slope.

FASTER AND FASTER

1 *Ask an adult to cut out a strip of stiff cardboard to make a ramp. Make sure the ramp is as wide as the shoe box. Fasten a piece of cardboard to the ramp to form a catch.*

2 *Tape one end of the ramp to one end of the box, making sure that the ramp can be put at different angles.*

3 *Ask an adult to cut out a quarter circle from cardboard. With a ruler, protractor, and marker, mark every 10°. Cut small slits at each mark. Slot the catch into one of the slits.*

4 *Ask an adult to cut the top off the bottle and pierce a small hole in the lid. Cut a hole in a piece of cardboard to hold the upturned bottle top. Tape the cardboard to the top of the car. Tape over the hole in the bottle top and fill it with colored water.*

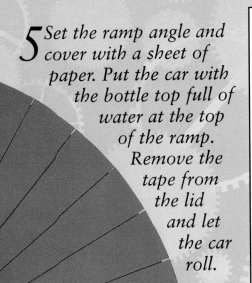

5 Set the ramp angle and cover with a sheet of paper. Put the car with the bottle top full of water at the top of the ramp. Remove the tape from the lid and let the car roll.

LITTLE CAR, BIG CAR

Repeat the project, this time with a heavier car. Does this difference in weight make any difference to the rate of acceleration and the gaps between each of the drops?

WHY IT WORKS

You will see that the spaces between drops become greater as the car moves down the ramp. This is because the car is accelerating, covering a greater distance between the release of each drop. Repeat the project on a steeper slope. The gaps will be even greater, as the car accelerates at an even faster rate.

FINDING OUT MORE

ACCELERATION This is the rate at which an object moves faster and faster. *Compare different rates of acceleration in the project on pages 28-29.*

AREA This is the amount of space that an object covers. *Turn to pages 10-11 to see how to make your own area grid to find out the area of different shapes.*

CENTER OF GRAVITY This is an invisible point on an object through which the weight of the object is said to act. *Find the center of gravity on a variety of different shapes in the project on pages 20-21.*

DENSITY This is how compact a substance is. Density is measured by the amount, or mass, of the substance that occupies a certain volume.

NERVE SIGNALS

Nerve cells carry signals from your brain to all parts of your body. Signals can travel around the long nerve cells at an astonishing 100 yards per second.

DENSE PLANET

The planet Saturn has such a low density that a piece of it would float in water. A similar chunk of Earth would sink.

Learn how to make your own hydrometer in the project on pages 14-15 and how to compare the densities of different liquids.

TALLEST BUILDINGS

The tallest buildings in the world are the Petronas Towers in Kuala Lumpur, Malaysia. These twin towers measure an amazing 1,476 ft high.

DISTANCE This is how far it is between objects. Distance can be measured in inches, feet, or miles. *Make a distance-measuring device on pages 6-7.*

GRADIENT This is a stretch of ground that slopes up or down. *Learn how to make a theodolite on pages 8-9, and use it to measure the angle of slopes.*

PENDULUM This is a weight that swings on the end of a long string or pole. *Find out how a pendulum can be used to measure time on pages 24-25.*

SPEED This is the rate at which an object covers a distance in a particular period of time. *Build a wind-speed reader in the project on pages 26-27, and compare the different speeds of the wind.*

VOLUME This is the amount of space that an object takes up in three directions, called dimensions. *The project on pages 12-13 shows you how to find the volume of different objects.*

BREATHING IN

Your lungs are two spongelike organs inside your chest which fill with air every time you take a breath. Everybody needs air to survive. When you take in a very deep breath, your lungs can hold more than 8 pints of air.

INDEX

acceleration 28, 29, 30

acres 10

angles 8, 9, 28, 29, 31

area 10, 11, 12, 30

balance 18, 19

center of gravity 20, 21, 30

circles 7, 9, 10, 22

clocks 22, 23, 24, 25

deceleration 26

density 14, 15, 16, 30

depth 12

dimensions 12, 31

distance 6, 7, 8, 12, 26, 29, 31

friction 25

gradient 8, 31

gravity 16, 17, 20, 21, 23

grids 10, 11, 30

height 8, 10, 12

hourglass 22, 24

hours 24

hydrometer 14, 15, 30

inches 6, 7, 10, 11, 31

length 10

measuring wheel 6-7

miles 10, 31

minutes 23, 24

molecules 14, 15

pendulum 24, 25, 26, 31

pivot 19, 20

plumb line 9

radius 7

scale 16, 17, 27

seconds 24, 25, 30

slopes 28, 29, 31

speed 26, 28, 31

squares 10, 11

surveyors 8, 10

theodolite 8, 9, 31

time 22, 23, 24, 25

volume 12, 13, 30, 31

weight 16, 17, 18, 19, 20, 21, 24, 29, 30, 31

wheels 6, 7

wind 26, 27, 28, 31

yards 6, 7, 10, 30